I'm not telling you!

Poems by Rachel Rooney

Illustrated by Hannah Bryan

Rabbit
Press

To Bryan Rooney and Roger Stevens for their encouragement and support
- Rachel
For Anthony Bryan L.Y.T.P. - Hannah

Copyright © Rachel Rooney 2004
Illustrations Copyright © Hannah Bryan 2004

ISBN 0 952654 2 1

First Published 2004 by
RABBIT PRESS
Sidegate Cottage
Northiam
Rye
TN31 6JP

LEGAL NOTICE

Printed and bound by Anthony Rowe Ltd, Easthoourne

Contents

O, the wonderful shape of an O

there's no other letter that's rounder or better with neither a stop nor a g...o see the wonderful shape of an o it's just a continuous flow

Riddle

What words are teasing
annoying, displeasing?
What's sure to put you in a stew?
What makes you cross when
your brain's at a loss for
the answer?

(I'm not telling you!)

Epitaph for Humpty Dumpty

Beneath this wall there lies the shell
Of someone who had talents.
But (as you can probably tell)
One of them wasn't balance

Warning

Beware wearing knickers with tightened elastic
While eating a large bowl of prunes.
The consequence of this is really quite drastic
Your bloomers swell up like balloons.
The warm air inside them will cause you to rise
And you'll helplessly float to the sky
A large crowd will gather to shout up advice

PULL 'EM
DOWN!

TAKE 'EM
OFF!

DON'T BE
SHY!

Never, Never, Never

Wear wellies when you're swimming
Or put jelly in your hair.
Brush your teeth with chilli pepper
Or tease a grizzly bear.

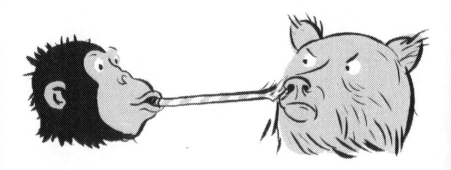

Don't ever think of sitting
On a mountain of red ants
Unless, of course, you want to learn
The itchy - scratchy dance.

Don't put stickers on your knickers
They'll come off in the wash
And never ask a hippo
for a friendly game of squash.

Playing catch with your dad's cactus
Is really not that clever.
Oh, and sniffing his old trainers
Is another triple never.

You can ignore these warnings
But there's one thing you should know
There's nothing more annoying
Than the words I TOLD YOU SO.

The Inspection

The day the in-spectres turned up here
We knew it was going to be tough.
The problem was that our behaviour
Was simply not dreadful enough.

The headless headmaster took action.
He hatched out a plan for the school
And passed it around in a leaflet
Entitled Guidelines for the Ghoul.

Your wailing is weak and infrequent
Your walking through walls could improve.
I'd like to hear more creaking handles
I'd like to see more objects move.

You must make more effort to vanish.
At least, slowly fade out from sight.
I don't want to see you in lessons
Unless your appearance is right.

The way that you play in the playground
Is really not shocking me much.
Try harder to creep up on classmates
And grab with a cold, clammy touch.

In PE, you must wear the full kit
So here's a reminder once more
Just slip on a white sheet with eye holes
And chains that reach down to the floor.

We followed these guidelines with gusto
Each time the in-spectres were there.
The head (and his body) were dead pleased
He literally floated on air.

We thought they'd be here until Friday.
But on Monday at quarter to two
They ran out the school gates in terror
I think we impressed them. Don't you?

A Song to Annoy Parents When Visiting a Museum

(To the tune of Oh I Do Like to be Beside the Seaside)

Oh I do want to be inside the gift shop.
I do want to be inside the shop.
I do want to wander down the aisles, aisles, aisles
Where the toys mount up in colourful piles, piles, piles.
I'll behave when I get inside the gift shop.
When I'm inside, this stupid song will stop
If you let me join the queue
For a souvenir or two
Inside the gift shop, inside the shop.

Spots Grow Anywhere

Spots grow anywhere
Any crevice where there's hair
Under fringes, in disgrace
In the middle of your face.
Some are solo inflammations
Others forming constellations.
Yellow headed, ripe for squeezing
Stubborn red ones made for teasing.
Spots are mean, they're diabolical
To the unsuspecting follicle.
Just beware 'cos they don't care.
Spots grow anywhere.

Creature Speak

The Worm's Turn

I once lived with my owner.
Then he chose to set me free.
He fell down in that hole he dug.
And now he lives with me.

Lice are Nice

Head lice are not loners
We're quite a friendly bunch.
That's why we swap our owners
When they sit down for their lunch.

Quiet Observation

If humans shed their skin, like us
Imagine how they'd moan and fuss
And think of what a meal they'd make
When eating dinner like a snake.

Don't Move the Goalposts

Don't move the goalposts.
Leave them as they are...

Well, maybe this much wider.
Now you've gone too far.

In a bit more. Stop.
Okay, that'll do...

No! You can't wear your jumper
Unless you swap it for a shoe.

What d'you mean you're cold now?
You always have to moan!

Don't go. I didn't mean it.
I can't play on my own.

Superstitious Sayings

Step on a crack
Break your mother's back.
Trip on a stone
Break your own.

See a penny, pick it up
All the day you'll have good luck.
Keep on looking, lucky kid
Hopefully you'll find a quid.

An apple a day
Keeps the doctor away.
Unless you're a pet
Then it's a vet.

Monday Morning

Hot head, Mum tuts.
Into bed, no buts.
Fresh sheets, warm drink.
Want a treat, Mum winks.
Fake sleep, Mum goes.
Sneaky peep, tiptoes.
Channel flick, key turns.
Up quick! Mum returns.
Knocks twice. Here we go
Choc-ice, Beano.
Head felt, asked how
Temperature normal now.
Later on, practise cough.
(Radiator turned off.)

Mrs Von Pugh

Let me tell you the story of Mrs Von Pugh
A teacher so fierce she could scare off the 'flu.
Her hair's like a jungle, I'm sure that a crow
Could nest there all summer and no one would know.
Her eyes are quite beady, like little squashed flies
But they work even better than highly trained spies.
Even when she is standing, her back to the class
She sees all the scribbly notes that we pass.
Her ears are like radar, they hear every sound
From whispers and giggles to worms in the ground.
Her nose knows exactly which smell comes from who.
She can sniff out a sweet from ten metres – it's true!
The work that she gives us would baffle Einstein
Like the square root of sixteen, divided by nine
Times three, add on twenty, and that's just the start.
We then have to learn all the school rules by heart.
And if we dare break one, we pay for our crime
By spending a week doing maths at playtime.
You may think I'm lying, just messing about
I don't need to prove it, I'll let you find out.
Our teacher is leaving - Yes Mrs Von Pugh
Has a job at your school, in your classroom, with you!

What am I?

Line
Dot
Cold
Warmer
Hot!

The Poem and the Poet

The chicken comes before the egg
A frog before its spawn
The plant must come before the seed
And deer before their fawn
But mums come after boys and girls
As if you didn't know it!
So can you tell me which comes first
The poem or the poet?

Answer: The poem (Because m comes before t in the alphabet)

A Written Apology

Believe me when I say I didn't lie
My answer to your question is a No,
I didn't. Cross my heart and hope to die.

My plane was wonky. That's what made me cry.
Yours turned out better. I admit it. So
Believe me when I say I didn't lie.

It looked realistic, good enough to fly.
You said I meant to crash it, even though
I didn't. Cross my heart and hope to die.

I tripped and fell and that's the reason why.
It was an accident; a drop, not throw.
Believe me when I say I didn't lie.

I could write - Stick a needle in my eye.
But I'll be honest just before I go.
Believe me, when I said I didn't lie
I didn't cross my heart or hope to die.

(I crossed my fingers.)

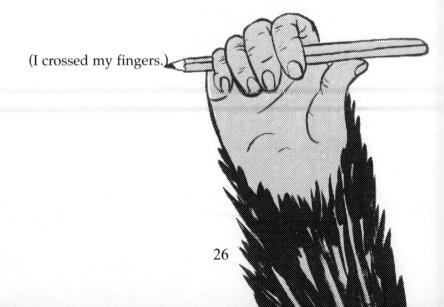

The Trouble Is...

Like jigsaw pieces from a different box
Like faulty plugs that have a broken pin
Like some odd key that won't undo the locks.
The trouble is... I don't fit in.

Like heavy black bin-bags to empty or
Like muddy balls and boots when adults shout
Like empty bottles lined up at the door
The trouble is... I am left out.

But unlike jigsaw pieces, plugs or key
And all those other things I mentioned there
I'm not an object. I can think and see.
The trouble is... I just don't care.

PROPERTY FOR SALE

Two houses up for sale.
One stick, one straw.
Both self-assembly.
See pig next door.

Lonely Heart

Handsome, lean wolf
Likes acting and cooking
Tired of old grannies
Is currently looking
For lady in red
With plump and soft skin
To share walks in the forest
And cosy nights in

Three Little Goldfish

1
I was just messing,
practising passes.
Nobody told me
how breakable glass is.

2

You needed fresh water,
but then I forgot
that C stands for Cold
and H stands for Hot.

3

I didn't feed you.
Nor did my brother.
Both of us thought
You were fed by the other.

Christmas Song

We wish you a hairy kiss, Miss.
We wish you a hairy kiss, Miss.
We wish you a hairy kiss, Miss.
    And a bottle of beer.

Good tie strings we bring
    To you and your bin.
We wish you a hairy kiss, Miss.
    And a bottle of beer.

Stocking Surprise

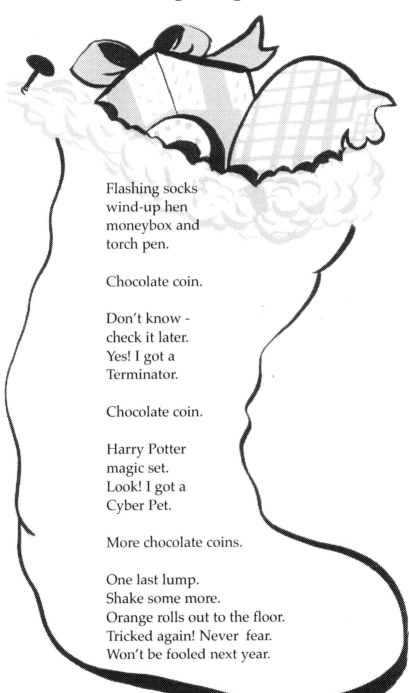

Flashing socks
wind-up hen
moneybox and
torch pen.

Chocolate coin.

Don't know -
check it later.
Yes! I got a
Terminator.

Chocolate coin.

Harry Potter
magic set.
Look! I got a
Cyber Pet.

More chocolate coins.

One last lump.
Shake some more.
Orange rolls out to the floor.
Tricked again! Never fear.
Won't be fooled next year.

The Grumpy Shepherd

I didn't want to be a shepherd
Wearing itchy girly tights
Without any words to say.
At least the lowly ox
Got to stand up on a box
In the end-of-term Christmas play.

I didn't want to be a shepherd
With a tea towel on my head.
Feeling sheepish is not my style.
I should have been the star
Shining brightly from afar
And that's why I didn't smile.

Epitaph for a Poet who wrote a Cinquain

Poet
In Poet Tree
Juggled words in her head.
She lost her balance. Once living
Now dead.

The Modern Monster

This monster is a high-tech beast
man-made, an import from Japan.
A slim-line foe, no fur or slime
its skin, lightweight titanium.
And on it's flip-top swivelling head
an eye to spy on you. It knows
the paths you tread. It can communicate:
transmit, long-distance, video
to monster mates that wait in shops
while scheming silently by text.
Next thing, instead of feeling fear,
you've fallen for that charmed ring tone.
And find one sitting in your palm
a dreaded monster mobile phone
demanding to be fed.

Three Monkeys

See No Evil didn't see
what Hear No Evil did.
He ran off to the jungle,
closed his eyes and hid.

Hear No Evil didn't hear
what See No Evil said.
He put his hands upon his ears
and hummed a tune instead.

Speak No Evil didn't speak.
He didn't shout or tell.
But there are other monkeys.
(And that is just as well.)

Making Friends

A new boy joined our class today.
His eyes are red, his skin is grey.
He will not come outside to play.
I think he needs a friend.

We set the goalposts on the grass.
We pick our teams, we strike and pass.
He's watching from behind the glass.
I'm sure he wants a friend.

A tackle causes injury.
Some blood is trickling from my knee.
I limp to class and there I see
The boy who has no friend.

He greets me with a sharp-toothed grin.
He licks his lips and helps me in.
Did I just hear him whispering?
Now you shall be my friend.

Hometime

It's nine past three.
Sixty-four eyes look at me.
No, sixty-two
Not Matthew
He hasn't learn to read my face.
He's got digital - a disgrace.
I reach to ten
The school bell sounds and then
Relief.
No more gluing, sticking.
Just me and the teacher

Ticking

Ticking

Ticking.

My Life as a Goldfish

TV	plant pot	books
TV	plant pot	books
TV	plant pot	books
TV	plant pot	books
plant pot	TV	books
plant pot	TV	books
plant pot	TV	books

plant pot
cat!

plant pot books
plant pot T V
plant pot books
plant pot T V
plant pot books
plant pot T V
claw!

The Everton Fan's Prayer

Our Rooney
Who art in Everton
Aloud be thy name!
Thy Skilldom come
Thy will outrun
On Earth
(As it is at Goodison)
Give us this day our
On the head.
And forgive them their messy passes
(As we forgive those who press up against us)
And lead us not into relegation
But deliver us a three - nil
For thine is the Skilldom
The Power and the Glory

Our Man

Monday 26th November 7.50pm

Our kid, Jamie
limps into view
Thin as a blade
(but not as sharp).
Fanfared by floodlight
and tannoys.

The swelling crowd
outstretch their scarves
They swallow him up.
Look there he is!
Spat out in centre circle
Our kid, Jamie,
gulping like a fish.

A smile breaks through
Wide as a goal.
His glasses glint,
reflecting glory
As he claps them clapping.
All Big Screen Magnification.

See the Captain wink at our kid, Jamie
Lurching forward to take a shot.
And again.
Go on!
And another
Yes!

Now back to centre spot.
Hand shakes
Pennants swapped.
Job done and off he goes.
Our kid Jamie, Premier Mascot
Looks behind, one last time
And waves to the world.

Jamie Delaney, Premier Mascot

Jamie Delaney limps into view
Thin as a blade and polished like new.
Fanfared by floodlight, tannoy and cheers
Comes Jamie Delaney, verging on tears.

The spectators swell, their banners held proud
For a moment he's lost, swallowed up by the crowd
Spat out centre circle, like a fish close to death
Stands Jamie Delaney, gulping for breath.

A grin breaking through, it's as wide as a goal
As he joins the applause and is part of the whole.
Reflecting the glory through well-dusted specs
Magnification with big screen effects.

With a wink from his hero, he follows the team
To the end of the pitch and the start of his dream.
For what seems forever, there's nothing at all
Just Jamie, the Captain, the grass and the ball.

But time's nearly up, one last duty outstands
The swapping of pennants, the shaking of hands.
Now Jamie Delaney leaves, fear overcome
Looks back for the last time and waves to his mum.

On the Way to School

I collect my own good luck.
Look out for yellow cars
Kick stones in drains, first time,
And touch the wooden-only gates
Of houses passing by

I'll be all right.
The lights have changed from green to red
Before I count to ten.
And still the flashing man is bleeping
As I step up on the pavement

I've made my own good luck.
I'm clutching fistfuls of the stuff.
Maybe this time there's just enough
To keep me safe.
To keep those bullies waiting

My Love is Like Chad Muska

I really cannot stand this stuff
This mushy hearts and flowers guff.
My love is like a red, red rose...
Pur-leeze!

Now, I'm not averse to verse
Don't get me wrong, there's worse
But this gets up my nose
It makes me sneeze.

So if you need to liken me
To something, via poetry
Remember this – I'm not some Romeo;
Give me talk of Tony Hawks or
Say I'm like that skateboard pro
Chad Muska
When you see me take a cool 5-0.

Try - Your Tail Grab really grabs me
Your Three-Sixty Flip just grips me.
When I watch you on the half pipe
It's a laugh. Yeah, you're just my type

Something like that would be all right
I suppose.
You might even get a name check
Get a chance to flex on my deck.
And then later on
Well, later on...
Who knows?

Boy in the Gas Mask

I saw him again last week,
His dark, close-shaven hair,
Pale legs beneath his chair
And a glimpse of a cheek.

Just a flash of a face
As he fumbles in his lap,
Pulls clear a jumbled strap
And fixes it into place.

I see that Mickey Mouse leer,
That rubbery snout disguise
And behind those goggled eyes,
A snapshot of his fear.

He crouches to the floor
Head low, grey bottom braced
Like a rodent trapped, out chased.
Last moments caught once more.

The Statue

He stands by day, plinth high
Once real, important, maybe even kind
Inviting the girl to climb.

Foot into stone into knee
Hand in iron hand
She clasps on to him
For that last stretch up.

Here, now, giddy flesh
Pressed against metal
She's the biggest thing alive.

At night, he wakes in purple light.
To see the girl, hurrying past
Head to earth, breathing fast.
Alone.

As iron lifts from stone
She stops, turns
Freezes him with her stare.

The Bench

I carved the letters deep with pride.
I scarred the rotting pine.
And now we lie here side by side
Your first name touching mine.

The rain may fade my traces and
The frost may blur your form.
But couples in embraces
Will keep our winter warm.

Defending the Title

I am the word juggler.
I juggle the words
like swords.
I slice sense
with poetic licence.

I am the letter mover
the metre lover.
Like rhyme
I time this
for poetic justice.

I am the brain rattler.
Shaking ideas
like dice.
A notion
in poetic motion.

I am the verse-making
rule-bending defender.
Beginner
and ender.
I am the poet king.

A Greengage is a Type of Plum
(a true story)

A greengage is a type of plum
I know this fact because my mum
brought home a sack full of the stuff
'Well you can never have enough
of fresh fruit for the family,'
she said, 'Especially when it's free.'
That night we ate them ripe and raw.
Then finding there were plenty more,
decided that she ought to try
a recipe for greengage pie.
And as the sack was hardly dented,
other puddings she invented.
Crumble, jams and roly-poly
bakes and cakes were served up solely
for our pleasure. But no thanks
were given by her hungry ranks.
Worse than this, we soon grew tired
of that taste, once quite admired.
On day eight to our displeasure
after dinner, in great measure
we received, against our wishes
stewed greengages served in dishes.
My father, not a man to grumble
was overheard to softly mumble
Oh no, it's not those things again
My mother didn't answer - then
stood up, and walking to his chair,
she raised his serving in the air,
and calmly without warning tipped
it from above. The warm plums dripped
all sweet and sticky from his brow,
upon the table, dish-less now.
Mum returned back to her seating
and resumed her silent eating.
Dad went to wash, while leaving us
to eat our pudding without fuss.

There is no moral to this tale
of greed or gratitude or scale.
These things apply, but my point is,
that I'll remember in a quiz
this fructal fact (all thanks to mum)
A greengage is a type of plum.

Counting Days

It's been six days, I've kept my silence well.
I give a yes or no, a stunted phrase.
My mother sighs, I don't think she can tell
The anger's gone. I'm simply counting days.

I didn't wipe the crumbs up, words were said
Then later screamed behind the bedroom door.
What started off as fussing over bread
Became a full blown mother-daughter war.

The bread's gone stale. My mother cannot wait
She asks me why I'm choosing not to speak.
I hesitate and shrug. I calculate
That I can hold my silence for a week.

A Sad Ending

A cynical man from Mauritius
Thought it foolish to be superstitious
When a black cat passed near
He stood firm, without fear
(What a shame that the panther was vicious)

About the author

Rachel Rooney

Rachel was born in Essex but now lives in Brighton with her three sons, three dogs and a cat. She trained and worked as a Primary and Special Needs teacher but since being bitten by the 'poetry bug' two years ago, now spends most of her time writing (or thinking about writing) poetry.

She has already had a number of poems published in children's poetry anthologies but this book is her first solo collection. She is currently studying poetry at Sussex University while working on her second collection.

About the illustrator

Hannah Bryan

Hannah has worked as an illustrator for over 10 years. Her pictures have been used as book covers, in magazines and brochures. As well as illustrating, Hannah teaches at the Camberwell College of Arts. This is the first time she has worked on a book for children.